Fiction Inc.

Mat de Melo

typewriter edition

ISBN 13: 978-1-7322497-8-3

All books published by nova ink printhouse

nova
ink
printhouse

SUBCULTURE BOOKS

Trademark cinematic,

montage poetry

Acknowledgment

A special thanks to the
typewriter punching poets.
To the midnight idea makers.
The stage-hungry theatre
players, and to anyone who's
ever wanted to rewrite the
world. To the tortured artists
and misunderstood geniuses. To
those who trust in the power
of unfiltered expression,
and the magic of words.

This one's for us.

I saw the angel in
the marble, and I
carved until I set
him free.

    - Michelangelo

Fiction
Inc.

ACT I

Scene 1

> An arthouse
> theatre.

The lights go down, and the curtain goes up. The main character emerges from the stage, then he reads his monologue to the theater.

MILO: Come rain or shine, or whatever happens, our intentions are made of gold,

and our advantages a built-in
tragic flaw. What romantic
ideas, to want and not have.
To make happen what is not
there. Is there no blueprint,
no handbook to This?
Nevermind the raindrops.
Put your raincoat on and
have no worry. The night
is almost here, and later
on, you and me will be
over the moon.

        To the projector
      beam.
What strange sensations to
have all the answers, to
see the world in color,
and have all that matters.

The storybook motion
picture moves 24 frames
per second, but this
somewhat fantasy is a
slow reveal.

> Juno is onstage with
> a roll of tape.

JUNO: You may bring the
house down.

MILO: Maybe, maybe not,
but that's no matter.
One day everyone'll have
read the words, ... *a
tragicomedy.*

JUNO: You'll be the toast
of the town, the matter of

the moment. It is on,
and anyone who's anyone'll
be there.

  Juno turns the power
  off on the stage.
  It is dark except for
  the exit light on the
  door. Milo puts his
  coat on, and he and
  Juno exit the stage.

Scene 2
Apartment 2e, Bairro Alto.
On a gray wool rug.

  Milo read Shakespeare in
  the dark, and Juno held

a lantern to the book.
*"Four days will quickly
steep themselves in
nights; Four nights
will quickly dream
away the time."*

Juno has an
idea.

JUNO: Is there no
antidote?

MILO: Maybe, maybe not.

JUNO: Maybe, in another
world.

> Later on.
> Milo has a reference
> of anecdotes and
> ideas, and Juno opens
> the memo book onto a
> random idea.

JUNO: **A literary character description**

Character One, the PoetWarrior.
The Prometheus of words,
who gave fire to humankind.
He is the bringer of poems.
With every verse, he makes into
reality what is not yet real.
Character One uses words as
both a sword and a shield.
His words echo through Bairro
Alto, a call to arms for

anyone who refuses to be
muted by the ordinary.

Character Two is the goddess
of ideas, and the prophetess
of talent. Unlike Cassandra,
whose predictions were true
and not believed, character
two's predictions are
together true and believed.
She sees the dormant
superpowers in everyone,
and therefore a muse for the
poetic rebellion. Character
Two summons character One
whose ideas blur the line
between reality and fiction.
Her character is unmistakable
and understood by everyone

in the theater where the
restrictions of time and
space dissolve on the stage.
Character Three is the
godfather of virtue.
He brings magic through
theatre. He is the producer
of art and the revolt
against the ordinary.
He rouses the masses
to make things.

Character Three is the
forebear of a generation.
He fuels the rebellion
with a hallucinogenic
elixir of good ideas.

Character Four: The Icarus
of rhyme and rhythm, he is
driven by excitement, and
therefore the rebellion
against the mundane.
He continues to push the
boundaries of physics and
dares everyone to make the
most of everything, and
much like character one,
he risks flying too close
to the sun of his
own genius.

MILO: What divine
interpretation.

JUNO: Is there more?

MILO: There is, and you
have a part in this drama.

JUNO: Who am I?

MILO: The oracle of ideas.

      Juno climbs onto
      a ladder.

JUNO: The die has been
cast, let us make it
happen.

      Dissolve to the
      theatre.

Scene 3
    Milo is on stage.
    The projector is on,
    and he reads his
    monologue to the
    theater.
MILO: **A prologue to this**
What is more than this,
than he who understood he
could have whatever he
wants, and who wholly
understood that there is
such thing as magic.
What is more is he who
has a novel idea and is
rejected, who rejects the
academic conventions and
challenges the established
standards. More is a

polymath on a rooftop in
Bairro Alto who launched
flyers from a cannon onto
the late-night caféhoppers
on Rua da Rosa, and
therefore began an
authenticity revolution.

More is Juno whose work
was to make an outline,
and color it in. More is
the anonymous wordsmith who
glued montage poems onto
bus stops in Barcelona.
More is the antihero's
overdue arrival, and a
shadowy, legendary mythos
whose superpower is

whatever he puts down on
paper happens to him.
More is the sun and the
moon and the stars, and
whatever glues it all
together. More is fiction.
More is over the rainbow.
More is on paper, and
somewhere out There.
More is whatever you make
it, and there is more to
unfold. Less there be
little green monsters.
Lest there be no time.

Scene 4
        Backstage, near the
        soda machine. Juno and
        Milo have a cola on a
        gray wool rug.
MILO: Words words words,
all I have is words.

        (Lighting a cigarette)
JUNO:
        You have been under
        a magic spell.
        Probably forever.

MILO: And so here I am,
on the floor with you near
the Coke machine holding
the Universe together with
words on paper and glue.

JUNO: You were nominated
for exactly that reason.

(Milo pauses)
MILO: There's the rub,
to have and not be the
part. On the stage, when
the lights go down and the
theatre is ultraviolet blue
there is an understanding
that what you see is
fiction, but there is
more than meets the eye.

JUNO: What's more?

MILO: To have an antidote
to time, to slow down,
and not be so romantic.

> Milo has a yellow-lined
> *idea book* with the
> words, *Act 2, the
> goodnight monologues.*

JUNO: Read it tomorrow,
on stage and with the
projector on.

> Exit Milo and
> Juno.

> Later on.
> Milo is on Rua de
> Andrada. He passes the
> opera house, then the
> cafés on Rua Garret.
> He slow-walks to the
> *Academia de Belas Artes*,
> and a round starry dot

rockets through the
mesosphere. He pauses,
and there he has a somewhat
minor revelation, that to
have an antidote to Time
he'd have to learn to defy
gravity, and move the speed
of light.

Scene 5
Apartment 2e.
The radio is on.
He unfolds a note
paper, and he reads
the poem aloud.

MILO: **The La Luna monologue**

To whom is This for? Is
it the PoetRocketeer whose
ideas are too unconventional
for mainstream organizations,
who launched onto his
word machine at night
without worry or caution.

When does the poet get to
read his montage poem to
the Harmonists in a

coffeeshop in Barcelona?
The microphone is on,
and the misunderstood
have not had a turn.

Scene 6

    There is a Super 8
    projector on the floor.
    A montage of moving
    pictures projects onto
    a wall.

Superimposed onto the screen:
A blue and red Mini Cooper.
A mid-afternoon drive on the
Nacional 4. The Alentejo.
Late-summer haze. A yellow
grass field, and poppy

flowers. *Espanha*, 180
kilometers. An FM radio.
A copy of a *Hitchhiker's
Guide to the Galaxy*. A case
of gin and tonic in the back
seat near Juno. A paper map.
A 35mm camera, and a neon
green plastic water gun.
Juno and Milo and Bacchus
have a cigarette, and the
radio is on. Milo presses
the gas, and the threesome
zoom forward.

On the stage.
Milo has the microphone.
He reads a poem to Juno,
and to the theater.

MILO: Somewhere in
Barcelona, someone with an
overactive imagination is
all in on a poem. Tac tac
tac into the night, words
words words, until finally!
a boxed wine manifesto is
had. Into that, and from
here on a sub-genre without
a name. What began as a
poem transformed into a
remedy to commonplace
ideas, and therefore a
generation of malcontents,
a subgroup of bright young
things all in on an idea in
a novel. That the Universe
is ours to have, and the
passport to This is in our

denim blue pockets.
That there is stardust
in our DNA, and therefore
some magic is needed to
make it happen, and that
you and me and almost
everyone here has the
prerequisites to this.

JUNO: Encore, encore!

MILO: There *is* no encore.

    In a voice that could
    only be described as
    'chocolate marshmallow
    s'mores.'
JUNO: Then add more, and
rename your almost fiction,

storybook fairytale *In
Blue Ink.*

> The curtain
> closes, and Juno
> exits the stage.
> Milo walks over to the
> proscenium arch,
> and with no one there,
> he pretends to wear the
> curtain like a blue
> hooded cloak.

Scene 7

> In the projection
> room.
> Milo and Juno sit near
> the movie projector.
> There is a transistor
> radio on the floor,
> and it is on. The
> Kerosene Lantern radio
> show begins.

ON THE RADIO: Mythology 101,
an introduction. Achille's
fury, and near invulnerability,
except for his heel. Jupiter's
thunderbolts and lightening.
Hermes' messages, and Apollo's
golden chariot.

Enter Bacchus, who has
four entry passes to
the Tanqueray costume
set, in Cinema São
Jorge. OCT. 31. 20h.

BACCHUS: Four passes for
four Rocketeers.

MILO: Is there a password
to this?

BACCHUS: There is.
Then.like.fiction. It is
there in invisible ink.

JUNO: I have an idea for
a costume.

MILO: You're Juno,
you be you.

      (To Milo)
BACCHUS: There is a
thunderbolt, and a bow and
arrow in the wardrobe room.

        Milo and Juno and
        Bacchus put their
        coats on.
MILO:
      Let's be off. There's
      no time to lose.

Scene 8
Part 1. The pregame.

(Milo's apartment)
John Coltrane is on the
radio. There are pizza
boxes on the floor. Milo,
Juno, Bacchus and Sonny
have Pisco Sours on a
gameroom mesa in a
roundtable discussion about
all that is more, and all
that matters.

    Moving laterally from
    one to another,
    underneath a drop
    light, and in a
    cigarette haze.
MILO: Here's one: Distill
greatness into a single
soul.

JUNO: Leonardo da Vinci.
     Then Michelangelo,
     then Rafael.

BACCHUS: Then Shakespeare.

SONNY: For me, it's
Michelangelo. Then maybe
Plato.

MILO: Then who?

JUNO: The Impressionists.

BACCHUS: Then the
Romantics.

SONNY: Then Kerouac.

Then Miles, and there is
many, many more.

MILO: Then Pablo Picasso.

JUNO: To me, there is no
past or present in art?

MILO: Of the two, words on
paper or motion pictures?

JUNO: To me, motion
pictures.

SONNY: Then words on paper.

BACCHUS: I'd say the
movies. It is art, it is

fiction, it is moving
pictures.

MILO: I'd say the portable
typewriter.

> Juno telephones a
> taxi. Sonny has a
> bottle of pisco in a
> small travellers bag.
> A Mercedes-Benz taxi
> zooms in, and Milo,
> Juno, Bacchus and
> Sonny down their Pisco
> Sours simultaneously.

Part 2.
The Tanqueray costume ball.

    Enter Milo and his
    entourage.
There are blue and pink
confetti paper on the
floor. Everyone had a
costume, and anyone who is
anyone is there. The movers
and shakers. The movie
makers and theatre players.
The college undergrads from
UNova and ULisboa and
UCatólica. The Romantics.
The coffeeshop baristas,
and the neoimpressionists.

There were two gin
bars, two Espumante
bars and two round
chocolate cakes with
the words *'What
incantations may
come?'*

A nineteen twenties
jazz remix sounded the
theater room.

(To Milo)

MILO: The world is ours
to rewrite.

JUNO: It's your idea.

Juno whirls her
gin and tonic.

JUNO: When does the
curtain come up?

MILO: Tomorrow, maybe.

JUNO: Is everyone in
costume?

MILO: You and me and
everyone here has a part
in this motion picture.

JUNO: You are a patron
storyteller.

MILO: I am but an
apprentice.

>   Juno pretends to have
>   a microphone.
> JUNO: You are a romantic,
> just like me.

>   Milo disappears into
>   the theater. Enter
>   Bacchus and Sonny.
> BACCHUS: Hello, there!
> Where is Milo?

> JUNO: Round'n us some
> *espumante*.

>   Bacchus motions to
>   Milo.
> BACCHUS: Make it three.

> SONNY: Make it four.

>   Milo returns with four
>   bottles of espumante,
>   one in each hand, and
>   2 in his coat.

MILO: To err on the
side of caution.
Less there be more.

>   Milo pops the cork,
>   and it rockets into
>   the air.

MILO: Here's to the
malcontents.

JUNO: Then to what may be.
>   The foursome slam
>   their cups together.

SONNY: To the night.
May there be a confetti
paper supernova, and may
This be never-ending.

(Later on)

Juno is on the veranda with
the theater staff. Bacchus
is on the sofa near the
Tanqueray bar, and Milo and
Sonny amble round the room
with a 35mm camera. From
ten thirty on the festa is
in motion, and the music
booms through the woofers,
and there is a clock on
the wall, and at midnight
everyone there threw
confetti into the air.

The Polaris Dawn space
launch is on the radio, and
everyone gathered 'round to
listen, and for a least
that night there was a
unanimous sense that the
Universe was ours, and all
things were possible, and
at the same time, nowhere
else in the world we'd
rather be.

Three hours later.
Milo has a nylon string
guitar. He plays a goodnight
lullaby, and everyone in the
theater hummed the words, and
one after the other the
drowsy costumeballers

dissolve into the starry,
starry night.

> There is a blue and
> yellow overlay, and
> fade in to an
> apartment in Chiado.
> Milo is asleep on the
> sofa, and in the
> middle of a dream.

A midsummer montage

Spain, on the A-2. Milo is in
a '73 sunkissed merlot, Fiat
850. He is in a mustard-
yellow t-shirt. The radio is
on, and the windows are down.
He presses his foot on the
gas, and with Madrid behind

him, he vrooms forward.
Barcelona, 500 kilometers.

Scene 9
      Milo is on stage, and
      in costume, in an
      oversized wool coat
      and polyester shirt
      and blue checkerboard
      pants. Juno is on a
      ladder with a Kodak
      super 8 on Milo.
      He reads his lines to
      the theater projector.
MILO: A playwright is in
his apartment on a blue
portable typewriter.

10 poems and an
outline for a motion
picture.

(In a type-on effect)
The antihero. An answer to
superposition. How to slay
a dragon. When it rains, it
pours. Out of the blue and
into you. The mittens poem.
'Twas a merry Xmas. Buttery
popcorn and magic
mushrooms. The motion
picture theatre, and used
books in Barcelona.

The outline:
Red yellow blue, let's
take my car. Boxed

wine supermoon build
me a time machine.
Goodnight, goodbye,
I'd do it all over
again.

He subtracts the outline
from the machine, and from
then on theatre and fiction
and the Realworld dissolve
into one. What began as an
abstract idea is transformed
into an object in the
Realworld. On paper and on
stage he is invincible, and
he can do and be whatever he
wants. But in the Realworld
there is a tragic flaw, and

for every advantage,
there is a disadvantage.

Scene 10

Behind the scenes.
Milo and Juno are in the
wardrobe room. Juno is in
costume, and Milo is trying
on a wool coat.

Enter Bacchus like a
gathering storm.
He falls down onto the
clothes on the floor,
and in a melodramatic
tone, he reads the
memo to Milo and Juno.

BACCHUS: From the Bairro
Alto Messenger: Meta
Theatre to close in May.
From, the Evil Organization
co.

> A thundercloud
> seems to loom
> over the room.

BACCHUS: The memo was
taped to the backstage
door.

> There'll be no theatre,
> and there'll be no
> Lights and Sounds.

ACT II

Scene 1

    Nighttime, downtown
    Cascais near the port.
    Milo and Juno are in
    the car.

MILO: How awesomely the
sun does set, and for what?

JUNO: What's past is
prologue to this.
The sun has set,
but not on you or me.

MILO: It does not matter.

JUNO: It matters to me,
and it matters to you.
It matters to us, and
there's more of us out
there, in the backdrop,
waiting their turn. I know
because I have seen them,
in Barcelona and Rome and
in Bairro Alto, in the
coffeeshops, on the tram,
in the bookshops, in the
back of the room near the
philosophy books. They are
everywhere, if you know how
to look. Regular people
cannot see them because
regular people do not know

how to see things with
their big round eyes.

MILO: It goes against
everything.

JUNO: Then we must go
against the grain. You and
me must take it to heart.
Use it as gasoline. Words
are like grenades, fill
them with flowers, and
fuckin' kill 'em with
beauty.

    It is all you and me
    really have.

Scene 2

Apartment 2e.

Milo is on the sofa. On the
floor is act One. There is
an Iliad poster on the wall.
Milo seems to emerge from a
dream, and like fiction, he
has an idea. He folds act
One into paper airplanes,
and one by one he launches
the paper airplanes through
the open window and into
the night. Unbeknownst to
Milo, Juno is sitting in
the car. The paper
airplanes zoom through the
air and onto the Avenida.
Juno does what Juno does,
and "doth emerge from her

chariot," and like fiction,
saves every single one.

Later on.
Milo has a brown
rectangular box with the
words Save For Tomorrow.
In the box is an amateur
philosopher's almanac.
A tragicomedy, act 3 with a
parallel storyline with 2
different resolutions, one
tragic, and one not so
tragic. A transistor radio,
and a notebook with the
directions on how to build
a time machine.

He adds a Kodak
picture slide of him
and Bacchus and Juno
in his car and a poem
that read: distance
yourself from the
establishment, rebel
against the norm.

Scene 3

Time-lapse to the
theater. Juno is
onstage. Enter Milo
onto the set.

(To the curtains)

MILO: What goes up, must
come down.

(To Milo)

JUNO: You have done thee
well. You'd do even better
to know so. Such sweetness
is so uncommon, and to that
end you are bulging at the
seams. There is magic to be
had, so try again. You'll
make it happen.

MILO: Onto what theater?
There's no one here. The
curtain will come down, and
then what? Alas, to have a
pillow to dream on. To be
like the poster on the
wall, young and decadent
and bright.

JUNO: The corporations may
have the stage, but not our
ideas. That is on paper,
and with you. The hero in
fiction will be back, and
when he does he will return
with the sweetest vengeance.
He will save twilight. He
will have his golden hour.

MILO: With whatever words
leftover.

JUNO: They have left us
with no option but to do
whatever we want.

MILO: **Rewind the tape to act 1, scene 4**
In the dark the theatre
player bides his time. The
projector is on, and he
slow walks onto the stage.
There is no one here but
us, and no reason to be
afraid, because there is no
such thing as a 'phantom of
the opera'. That is, until
there is.

(To Juno)
BACCHUS: This is anapogee,
if there ever was one. It
is an intent to disrupt the
ordinary. More than words
on paper, a handbook for

the malcontent. To the
ones who dare, From the
ones who dare. There ought
to be a name for the cause,
and there ought to be a
superhero. He ought to be
true to his word, and a
giant amongst men. He ought
to be all in. He ought to
wear his colors, and he
ought to act as if he were
the difference.

Let us draw a line in the
sand. You cannot move from
your position. You cannot
back down here, and you
cannot erase not one word.
Let it be used as an

example for the good and
the bad and the divine.
Is there no time? To where
then goes the star of
the show, does he not
understand how important he
is? He may not have woken
from his sleep, but he must
have understood that life
is but a dream. He ought
to set his alarm. He ought
to move into the theatre,
and he ought to take his
sleepy ideas with him,
because nighttime is
almost here, and it's
time to be the part.

(To Milo)

JUNO: These boots are made for walking, and so are you.

To the projector

MILO: Is there no rhyme or reason to this, to fabricate what is not there?

JUNO: The gods have allowed you an unparalleled genius, use it to your advantage.

MILO: What menace the
time. Is there no wickeder
threat to this? Is there no
one worser?

JUNO: You have to make the
time. You have to have an
idea, and it has to be
larger than life itself.

MILO: Then like in the
motion pictures.

JUNO: More so than ever
before.

Milo has an idea.
MILO: There is option b,
to build a theater. Buy a

projector, stage lights,
and costumes. Then make an
ad. Make it a poem, then
make copies. Then glue
them onto coffeeshops
and theaters everywhere.
Begin in Lisboa, then
Porto. Then Madrid, then
Barcelona and then Rome.
Then Berlin, and then
Holland. Then Bogotá,
then Buenos Aires. Then
Hawaii, and then Nippon.

JUNO: I can make the art.

BACCHUS: I can make copies.

MILO: And I have the glue.

There is a paper
airplane on the floor.
Milo unfolds the
paper, and he reads
what is there.

MILO: Master your
superpowers. Learn to
think like you are it,
and there is more.

BACCHUS: It is not an
exaggeration, and nor is
it fiction, you really have
to be the metaphor, and do
what you have to do to make
it so. What's sad is you
and me and Juno are the
last of a generation, and
the theater is no more.

MILO: There's more of us,
somewhere out there.

>   Juno is on the ladder,
>   and Milo is near the
>   curtain.

>>   (To the theatre
>>   boxes)

JUNO: I want to return to
the past, and start over.
To the *cine-teatro*. To the
movie posters on the wall.
To the Moulin Rouge.
To Années Folles and the
cafés on Montparnasse.
To a 30 sqm apartment.
To the late-night
dialogues, and to the

nighttime. You have it in
you. You'll make it happen.

MILO:

    I'll need more time.
    I'll need a portable
    typewriter and paper,
    and I'll need some
    magic.

BACCHUS:

    You have all the words
    you'll ever need, each
    one worth its weight
    in gold.

JUNO: Did you take
precautions?

MILO:
    There were gargoyles
    everywhere, and it was
    not enough.

JUNO: You have a villa
in Spain surrounded by
grapevines. You have red
wine. Every August the gods
disguised as fireflies
visit you on the veranda.
You have a typewriter,
and you have paper. You
have a battery-powered
radio. What more is there?

    There are two theatre
    ladders onstage, and
    Milo and Bacchus climb

           onto the ladder

           near Juno.

MILO: Here's to whatever
this is. Here's to us.
To the melodramatic.
To what was, and to
bittersweet revenge.

BACCHUS: There is option b.

           To the theater, as if

           there is a tropical

           storm coming.

JUNO: There's enough bad
in the world. Let's be a
force for good, and blow
it all up.

BACCHUS: There's no time.

JUNO: There is time,
there's Maciuss.

MILO: On paper, maybe.

    Juno climbs down and
    onto the tape mark on
    the floor like this is
    her. big. moment.
JUNO: Who is Maciuss but a
make-believe character, a
regular superhero and a poet
and a muse. Exaggerate for
me what happens. Pretend
like you are on a stage.
There's the microphone,
read us a poem. Raise the
curtain, and bring the house
down. O captain, my captain,

we'd climb onto a
schoolhouse desk for you.
We may die here on this
hill, but then we'd live
forever.

Don't listen to the
antagonists, there'll be
more. And so do not worry,
you'll conquer the world
soon enough in your own
words, and in 24 frames
per second. But till then,
let us in on what makes
you you. Is it time,
or is it words on paper?

O pomegranate angel who
once upon a time in Lisbon

divided a Romã in thirds,
one for me, one for you,
and one for Calliope,
who used to carry a blue
WordMachine on mythology
making research projects.
Tell me how when you were
thirteen you used to
pretend you were a guardian
of the universe. Tell me
that you were not afraid of
the dark, and that there is
no such thing as monsters.
To the mind-wanderers whose
exaggerated ideas cannot
come soon enough, I have
thought so much about it.
Every poet has a muse, and
every superhero has a

limitation. That's why
everyone wants to know,
what makes you you. Is it
vengeance? Is it Love, or
the idea of it?

There is a 10am Renfe
to Hendaye. Bring the
antidote, and let's start
over. The bedtime story is
almost at an end, and you
are 43 y.o. Oh, but that's
no matter; you're young to
me, it's time that won't
stand still.

    (An applause)
MILO: Is there an
alternative?

BACCHUS: To be not normal
is a prerequisite. You
cannot have your cake and
eat it too.

MILO: I want to conquer the
world, and take it back from
the corporations and return
it to the malcontents.

BACCHUS: There is no such
thing. Not here. Not in
this time. Not to the
business makers.

MILO: There is to me,
and there is to you.

JUNO: Art exists because
it is necessary, and it is
always necessary.

      A dramatic pause.

MILO: You are a romantic
through and through.

JUNO: Is there no more
magic?

      (To Juno, on the
      floor)

MILO: The magic is in the
words. It is why raindrops
are blue. I'll put it on
paper, and you can
color it in.

(To Milo)

JUNO: You rubric how to be
superhuman. Sometimes I
think you are not of this
world.

Exit Bacchus, and
then Juno.

Milo turns to the
projection operator.
He says goodbye, and
one by one the lights
turn off.

ACT III

Scene 1

>A butterfly flutters
>its wings and causes a
>hurricane on the other
>side of the world.

>Nighttime.
>Wide shot of a movie
>theater in Bairro Alto.
>Then to Milo in the
>back of the theater,

underneath the projector
beam. He is in his seat
with a medium cola. The
words project onto his
plain white t-shirt.

In a succession of
retro colors, mandarin,
blue and brown.

*Introduction: To the idea
generation, an ethos, a
user manual for idea
makers. Make time for the
idea to flower, and see it
through to the end.*

Scene 2
     Three horizontal frames
     play simultaneously on
     the screen.

          Frame one.
Milo is at his typewriter,
all in on a promise he had
with the Universe. Tac tac
tac, he types into the
night. The words seem to
jump off the page until
finally, a metamorphosis
is had, and he has his
antidote to time.

          Frame two.
Juno is in her car at a
traffic light. The light

turns green, then yellow,
then red. Mozart is on
the radio, and Juno does
not move, and again the
light turns green, then
yellow, then red. This time
Juno presses the gas and
zooms forward.

Frame three.
Bacchus is on the sofa
with a Renfe ticket to
Barcelona, via Madrid.
He puts the ticket in
his pocket, then he put
on his coat.

Scene 3

A café on Rua Garret.
Juno is at a table in
the back. Milo is in a
blue flightsuit.

He and Bacchus
order a coffee.

BACCHUS: The theater
house'll be wreckingballed,
and then, the Meta will be
no more.

JUNO: What'll happen to us?

BACCHUS: We'll be returned
to the archives.

JUNO: What's option 3?

MILO: We'll need a new
theater, and more theatre
players, the ones who are
not afraid of monsters,
and who'll read Shakespeare
in the dark. We'll need an
idiot romantic. We'll need
lights and a projector and
an idea so unbelievable
it'll be almost impossible
hard to put into words.

JUNO: The magic is
wearing off.

BACCHUS: Maybe there'll
be another contract.

MILO: No. Alas, there's
no time.

Bacchus pauses.
BACCHUS: Here's to the
idiot romantics, who are
not afraid to try, and
sometimes make it. Who gasp
at the thought of losing
everything, and do it
anyway. Pay no attention
to uncertainty, and do not
worry. Put your ideas onto
paper and tread on with
what you have. All it takes
is time and pressure,
and you'll have your
revenge poem.

        Milo hands Juno a
        used book.

JUNO: What is it?

MILO: A handbook, on
monsters and daydreams
and nightmares.

JUNO: Who's the author?

MILO: An anonymous person,
although I'm not sure he
is a person.

        Bacchus stands up and
        climbs onto a chair
        like he is on a stage
        and like he has
        something important

to say. Everyone in
the café turns and
looks.

BACCHUS: To Milo-from one
dramatic to another.
The superhero in you will
return, and in that time,
you'll have learned that
you had it all along, and
like all superheroes you
will have learned how to
use it for good and on
whatever you want. In time
you will either succumb to
your vices and become the
villain or be forced to
choose between who you are
and what you really want.

> The 28 tram zooms in.
> Milo sees it as a
> call to action.

MILO: The curtain has
closed, and our late-night
show is over.

JUNO: Where to?

> A dramatic pause.

MILO: Rome. I have a
rendezvous with the gods.

> Milo and Juno and
> Bacchus make a circle,
> and what begins as a
> group hug ends in a
> curtain call.

MILO: Fare thee well.
May there be gold at the
end of the rainbow.

JUNO: Parting is such
sweet sorrow.

    Bacchus says goodbye,
       then he exits the
       café.

JUNO: Goodbye, Milo.

MILO: Goodbye.

Scene 4
Milo is in his car, full
speed down the Avenida.
He reaches a No Turn On Red
marker, and he turns onto
the theater nonetheless.
He steps out of the car
and onto the backdoor with
a heavy, iron sledgehammer.
He moves backward, then he
slams the padlock open.
Then he opens the door,
and enters the theater.

Milo slow-walks onto the
stage. He opens the curtain,
then he pauses, then he set
his attention onto the
theatre, onto the art on

the wall. All the muses
were there: Calliope, Clio,
Polyhymnia, Euterpe,
Terpsichore, Erato, Melpomene,
Thalia and Urania. He does
not say a word, and he does
not have to. He knows that
they know that his ideas are
on paper, and that he read
them often, sometimes to
La Luna, and sometimes to
a theater of three.

There is a box of theatre
posters on the stage. He
imagines a full house,
everyone dressed in
costume. Each one had
a Fiction Incorporated

program, and pocket
full of paper moons.

On stage, and in
costume, he reads
his avengers poem.

The dress code monologue

To anyone who was different,
who was pushed to the
fringe, had to conform
to normal ideas or leave.
Dress how you want to dress.
Be who you want to be.
Put your costume on, and
act like you want to act.
There is no option b, and
the ideas in our mind is
all we'll ever have.

The stage is set, and so
nevermind the raindrops.
Put your shoes on, and walk
in the rain. Do not lose
what makes you *you*. The
world is ours to have,
and when the curtain goes
up and the show is on,
be the counterpoison to
whatever wants to undo you.

    Is there such thing
    as magic? Maybe, maybe
    not. But we can
    pretend.

>   Milo pauses near
>   the curtain.

**Sweet Calliope, the words
don't come cheaply.**
Underneath the moonbeams
where you and me and
Bacchus had a gentlemen's
agreement, that I'd put all
that glitters and glows
onto paper, and that I'd be
allowed all the advantages,
and you'd have your
nighttime poems. To that
end, our work here is done.
The mandarin sun has set,
and what is left is a guy
on a stage in a Hawaiian
shirt. He is in costume,
and he has made good on his

agreement. How then does
he elude the melodramatic,
unless all the world's a
stage. It is then a goodbye
lullaby, a secret handshake
to theatre goers every-
where. Alas, the world
needs a redemption poem,
a call to action: Save the
movie house. Save theatre.
Save ideas.

(To the pretend
microphone)

**I am but a poet's
apprentice.** There is no
idea so unlikely, and no
one so crazy to have an
idea, and therefore
manufacture a world that
does not exist except on
paper. He'll exaggerate
every word, and lo! like
magic what is on paper
really does happen.
He may have to move the
speed of light, and he may
have to rearrange the stars
to do so, but he'll have
his midsummer night
anecdote. It may take

forever, but that's no
matter—one day he will have
his redemption, and it will
be thought of for all of
time, and it will never
really expire.

Milo turns to the theatre
exit onstage. There is a
30-watt light bulb. He
turns it on, and so when
there is no one there,
and so not to sabotage
the set, so the theatre
ghosts of the past could
play onto the night.

Write to us

nova ink printhouse
Rua de Alcamim, 21
Elvas, PT 7350-014

Mat de Melo
matdemelo.info

novainkprinthouse
@proton.me